Atlantis: An Elegy

Atlantis

An Elegy

George Peabody

Chapel Street Editions

Appreciation of Place

Chapel Street Editions exists within the unceded and unsurrendered territories of the Wolastoqiyik, Mi'kmaq, and Peskotomuhkati people. The work we do is born from the stories carried by this land and its inhabitants. The animals, plants, soil, water, and air make this place home for the Indigenous people, who belong to this land, for the descendants of those who took this land and made it a belonging, and for those who have since come from away. Chapel Street Editions holds a deep appreciation for our place within this land and the stories it tells. We honour the land's Indigenous caretakers and offer our gratitude for their wisdom and guidance.

First published in the *The Pottersfield Portfolio, Volume 5: Fiction and Poetry from Atlantic Canada 1983-1984*. Porters Lake, NS.: Pottersfield Press, 1984.

Copyright © 1979-83, 2022 by George Peabody
All right reserved

Published by
Chapel Street Editions
150 Chapel Street
Woodstock, NB E7M 1H4
www.chapelstreeteditions.com
chapelstreeteditions@gmail.com

ISBN: 978-1-988299-40-2

Library and Archives Canada Cataloguing in Publication

Title: Atlantis : an elegy / George Peabody.
Names: Peabody, George, author.
Description: A poem. | Previously published in Pottersfield portfolio, volume 5 (1983/1984).
Identifiers: Canadiana 20220151334 | ISBN 9781988299402 (softcover)
Classification: LCC PS8631.E225 A7 2022 | DDC C811/.6—dc23

Book design by Brendan Helmuth

Dedication

For those who resisted the rising of the water
and the loss of land and culture.

&

For Debrah Westerburg whose love of this poem
is surpassed only by my love of her.

Table of Contents

Geographic Note

Atlantis: An Elegy is set along the Wolastoq—also known as the St. John River—in the Canadian province of New Brunswick

Atlantis: An Elegy

Atlantis: An Elegy

I was a child before the Flood.

Our home was perched above the shore,
protected by a slope we burned
each year to force the phoenix grass
to lush and green profusion from
the ashes of its splendid death.

We flailed the edges of the flames
with spruce boughs which had banked the house,
and scrambled up and down the slope
between the lawn and water's edge,
dragging flaming cattail heads
to spread the fire out in lines.

A Rite of Spring I'd call it now—
as if the name defined the thing.

The water took that slope long since,
took the lawn and took the house,
took the cut-grass, took the trees,
drowned those trees that lined the shore—
water maples, ash and elm,
the willows bent like farmers' backs
to drop their seed into the flow
where ceaseless current spread their kind
from river's start to river's end.

I saw the seasons in that stream,
their stately whirl in spiral time
when ice would heave and crush itself,
defeated by another year's
conspiracy of sun and rain.

The freshet flush that followed full,
stained with the brown of forest roots,
the water spilling over banks,
embracing trees, caressing fields
with gentle, timeless, savage strokes.

We'd launch the boat my uncle built
and paddle till our arms were sore,
and still we'd dig and pull and watch
to see the trees slide slowly back,
to gain the slack of silver fields
where gullies ran like veins into
the labyrinth hearts of continents
unknown to other times of year.

One evening, not long after dusk
had merged the water with the sky,
we'd turned the boat to drift downstream
when from the darkness came the logs;
escapees from a bursting boom
a hundred miles or more away.

Gleaming brown in awkward herds
like river monsters out for fun,
they nudged our flanks, and we began
to draw them in; to guide them home—
flotsam, free foundation sills
that could be used to start a barn.

Matching adolescent strength
against the ancient freshet surge,
a little convoy inching in
as if to mock the springtime sight
of tugs that drew the cook-boats up
from winter berths beside the bay.

A string of beads in child-bright hue,
which pulled, reluctant, at the towboat's
stern in chocolate water churned
to violent froth by power hid
from eyes ashore where children watched
them disappear beyond the bend.

Great power oftentimes is hid,
and seldom can be understood;
not even when it's clearly seen.

As clear as float plane hung in sky
above the brown tumult of pulp
that scrapes against the river banks
like lemmings flowing to the sea.

As clear as paint spots on our logs
that marked them with a brand so deep
within our minds we set them free
when morning sun revealed the stain.

As clear as red-topped survey stakes
that sprout like toadstools on the shores
above the highest freshet marks:
auguries of the larger Flood.

I had not learned to read the signs.
I dreamed no cataclysmic dreams.
I knew the constancy of change,
certain and uncertain both;
the marks of life, of living things
that grow and die and are re-born
in cycles great and cycles small.

I watched the water rise and fall,
heard its voices change their call
from hour to hour, from day to day—
never silent, never still.

Even locked in Winter ice,
the hope of change was held by springs
along the shore, which kept it fresh
and undermined the solid shield
with sudden pools that threw up steam
like exhaled breath in frozen dawns.

At first the springs and then the pools,
and then the ducks on whistling wings
to bring the lurching seasonal change,
the freshet fury fast removed:
the breathy rush of thrill subsumed
in humble, magic, placid days.

To pole a boat past shallow shores
or ride an eddy up the stream;
to comb the banks for fiddleheads,
for bloodroot, or for adder's tongues;
to watch a muskrat's arrowhead
of water spread in lazy light;
to stay as still as standing stone
and watch a wood duck lead her brood
the little distance down the brook
from nest in tree to life afloat;
to see a sudden summer flood
sink aftergrass on intervales,
make roses shine beneath the boat,
their petals pale like faces drowned
though lovely still, and still alive.

These passing treasures of a week;
these lasting diamonds of a life.

To walk on sandy island soil
in the hush of green cathedral trees
where vines as thick as haywarp hung
from high above, as if designed
for use as swings; fixed so secure
the weight of two or even three
small boys, applied with running leaps,
would scarce produce the slightest give.

To pass to where at island's head,
against the first bulwark of trees,
the magpie freshet had for years
deposited its varied hoard
of cans and bottles, logs and bones—
a vast untidy mingled heap
of all that floated, cast ashore,
renewed and rearranged each Spring,
and yielding worthless valuables
to probing sticks and eager hands.

The triumph of discovery
outlives the finds; the ends grow pale
and indistinct, and disappear—
not so the means.

Experience remains the only jewel in all
the hoard, as slippery and as hard
to kill as eels we hooked for fun
on Summer nights when fire-light
had lured them close enough to shore.

In daylight other anglers came.

All Summer long we saw them stand
where ripples danced on gravel bars
and swing their supple bamboo rods
with flies they'd tied to fool the fish.

All Summer long the salmon came
and mostly spurned the offered bait
to jump instead in favoured pools
and flash like silver in the sun.

That Summer of my nineteenth year
I only had the old excuse—
I didn't know; I needed work;
I did what I was told, no more.

I learned the light precision touch
to snap the jaws of hoppers wide
and dump the concrete, fill the trucks,
which fed the cranes to build the dam—
the cranes that stood as herons stood
among the pools along the shore
when August sapped the river's strength.

Each Autumn sent those herons south;
or so I thought. One Winter though,
when clearing snow to make a rink
below the cove where ice was best,
I found a shape embedded there
beneath my skates; a shadow form
of blue-grey life. But real and sharp
as if entrapped by Winter's grasp
while eyes still sought for fish and frogs.

In dream I saw the cranes entrapped,
the concrete rising round their steel.

By Summer's end I knew for sure
that I would be no engineer.

I did not wait to see the Flood.

There was no sudden massive surge,
no panic-stricken human flight—
the gates were ceremonially closed,
like Kali's sacred strangling scarf.

The water gathered, dark and slow
to shroud the rubble heaps where homes
had stood—the amputated trees.

As false as fog it covered creeks.
A first and final tidal bore.
A flow not followed by an ebb.
Time turned back upon itself.
A single scene, forever fixed—
all is changed, and changeless now.

The sweeping curves that current cut—
geometry geological—
are broken by the human line.
The river chafes between its banks,
uninterrupted now for miles
before a bend that even man
could not erase, provokes a shift,
begins another sterile stretch.

The tourists stop at scenic spots.
Their cameras see the autumn hills
where maples watch their mirror selves
reflected in the lake below
like perfect ghosts those long-drowned shores
are still unwilling to release.

The gulls that once we hungered for
as solitary signs of Spring,
come now each Fall in crying crowd
to bleach the fields behind the plough
and float in mercenary flocks
between the bland amorphous shores
like strangers at a funeral feast.

The salmon ride upstream in trucks.
The water darkly slaps the steel
of temporary prison walls.
As blind as cave fish in that gloom,
they bump their boundaries, flex their fins,
and taste the staleness on their gills.

Perhaps recall the greenish glow
of ice-hung oceans left behind.
Or maybe dream of gravel bars
with depths of cool outside the sun
reflecting from the polished stones.

Along the turgid lake they pass,
unseeing and unseen. The bars
are drowned, and tourists come to cast
for bass, while sullen little waves
gnaw the shores with mud-stained teeth.

Lower Woodstock
Carleton County
Wolastoq Watershed
1979-1983

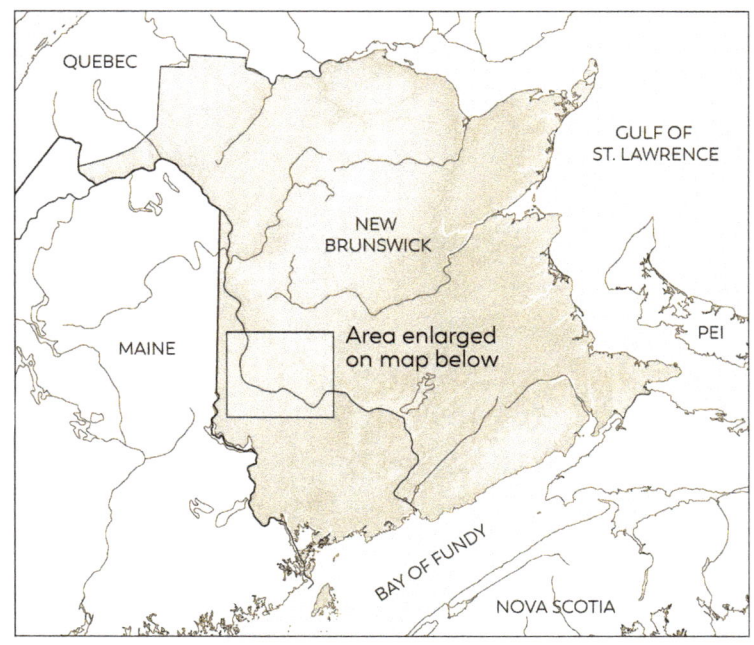

New Brunswick, Canada.

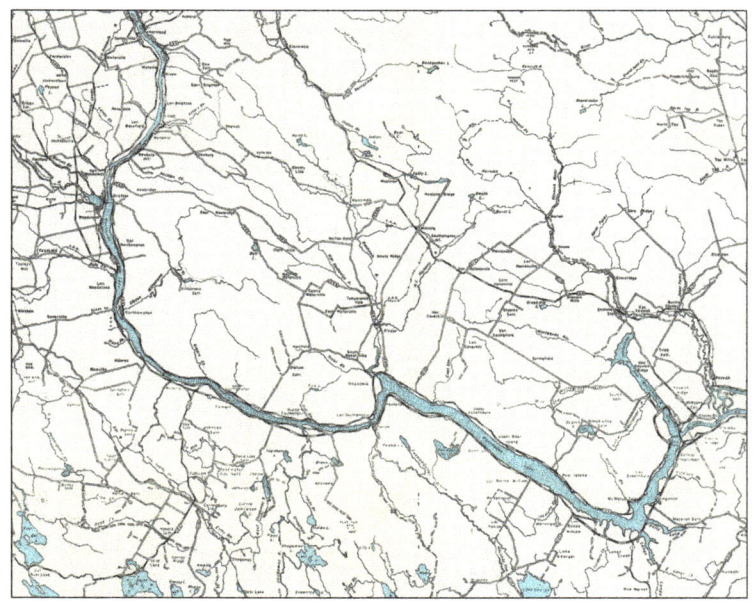

Portion of the Wolastoq affected by the Mactaquac Dam.

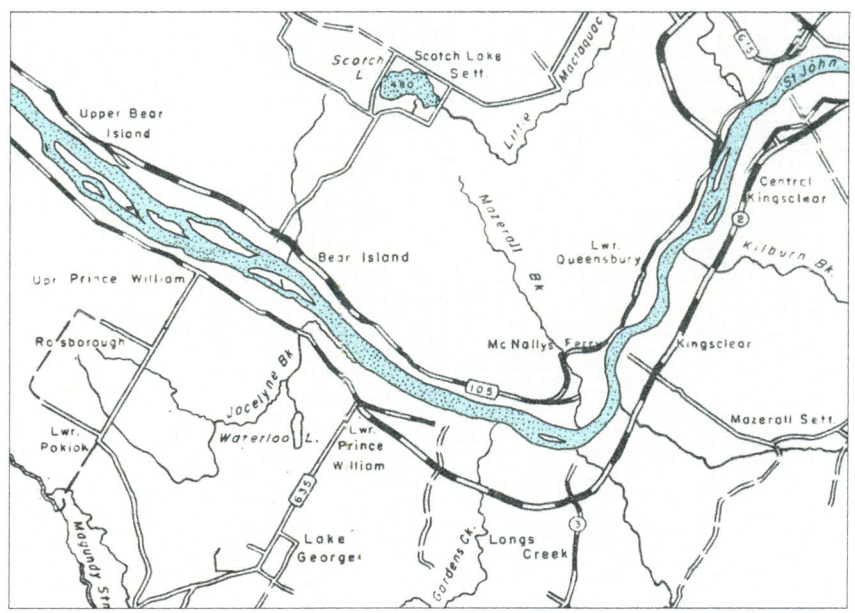

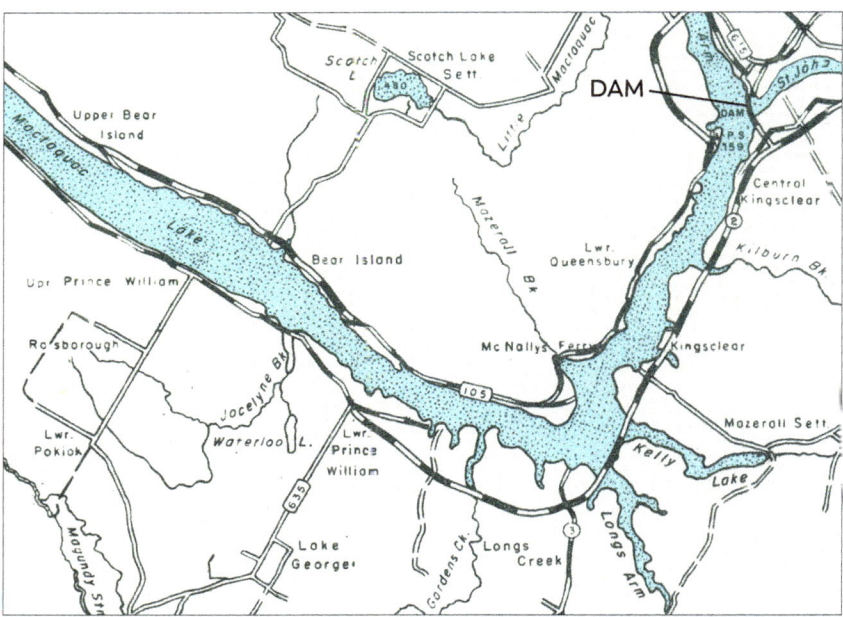

Details of the Wolastoq between Upper Bear Island and Kingsclear before and after the building of the dam.

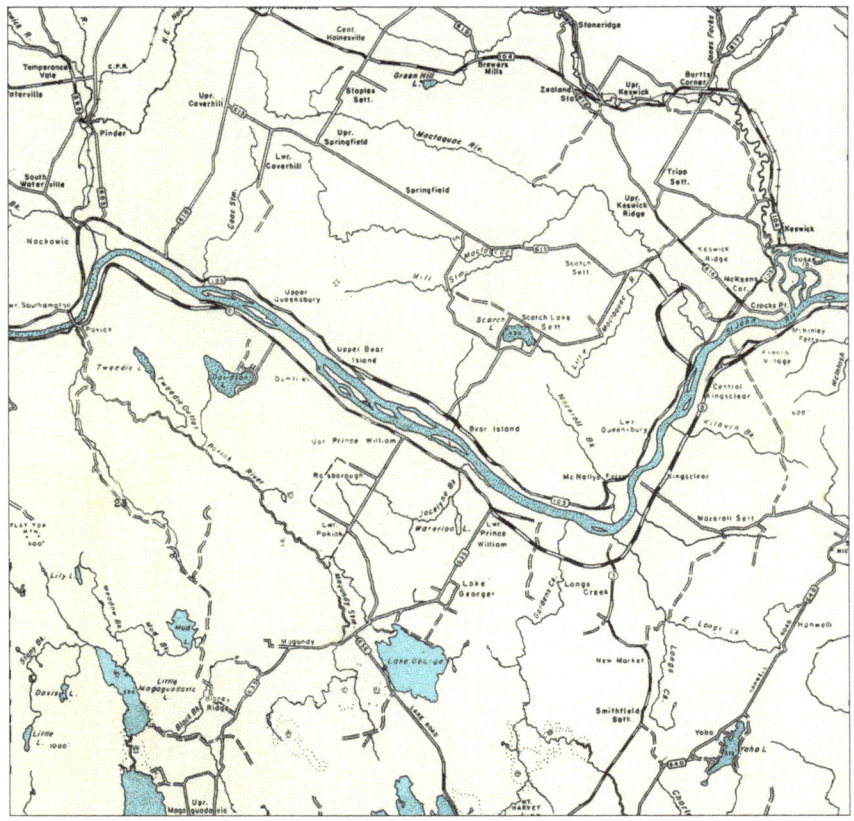

Detail of the Wolastoq between Nackawic and Kingsclear showing the original course of the river before the building of the Mactaquac Dam.

This visualization of the original shape of the river was created by referencing the pre-dam aerial photos used in the interactive online map made by Larissa Holman in 2014.

To view her map go to www.arcgis.com/index.html and type "Under the Mactaquac Headpond" into the search bar.

The roads on this map have not been restored to their original positions near the river. To see these and other features, such as farmland, go to the online map at the link above.

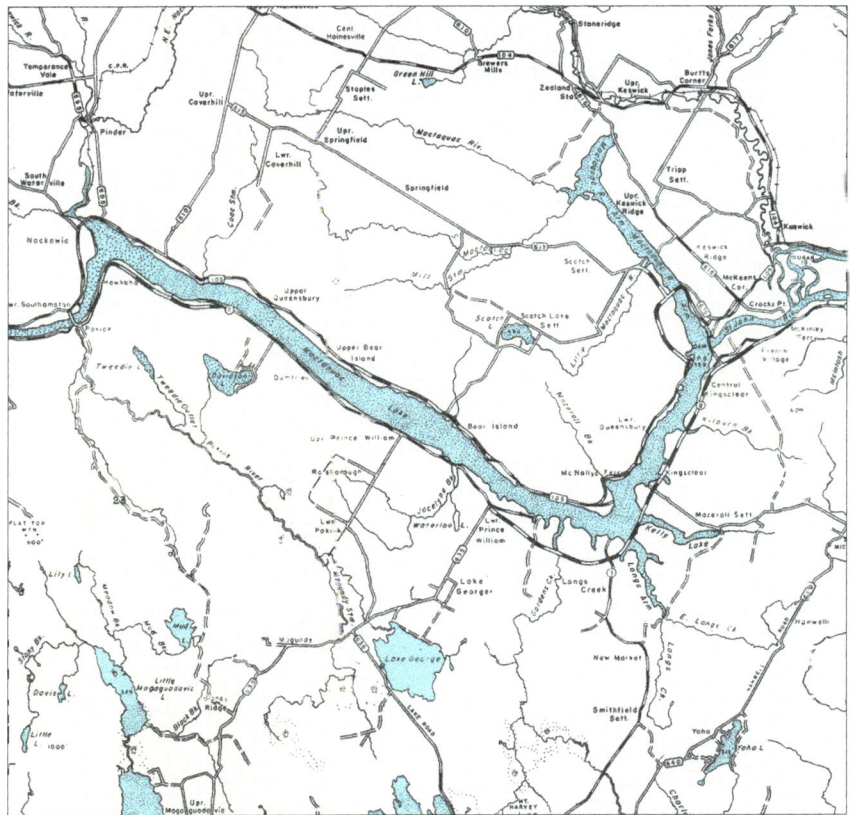

Detail of the Wolastoq between Nackawic and Kingsclear showing the flooding caused by the headpond after the building of the dam

The base map used to create these comparisons was published by the New Brunswick Department of Natural Resources in 1969.

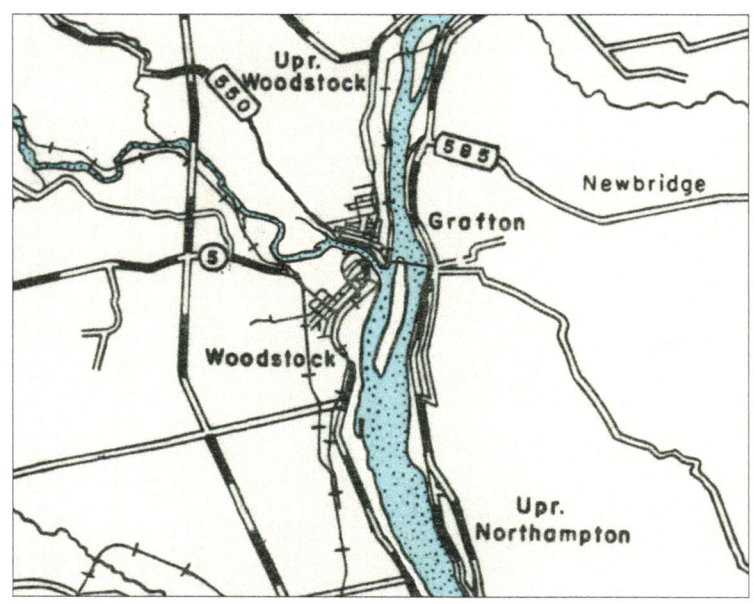

The Wolastoq near Woodstock and the author's home
before the Mactaquac Dam.

The Wolastoq near Woodstock after the Mactaquac Dam.

Afterword

Atlantis: An Elegy gives us a flagship poem for the memory of life along the Wolastoq before the building of the dam at Mactaquac.

Of all the mistakes made by the descendants of the Europeans who came to North America, perhaps none has been more dramatically destructive of natural abundance than the damming of salmon rivers.

The Wolastoq—also known as the St. John River—flows from northern Maine through western and south-central New Brunswick to the Bay of Fundy. Building a hydroelectric dam at Mactaquac in the mid-1960s destroyed the annual regeneration of salmon in the central watershed of the river. The annual salmon migration for upstream spawning had been a prime feature of the region's natural abundance for untold centuries. In addition, when the water rose behind the dam, intervale land long farmed went under and was lost to the local food economy. With one blow, Mactaquac Dam took out two major features of a sustainable, self-provisioning economy. What were they thinking?

We know what they were thinking because they told us. The boosters behind the building of the dam said it would create a corridor of industrial development and economic wealth comparable to the Ruhr River Valley in Germany.

Those were the days when it was imagined that prosperity meant developing an extraction-based, manufacturing, export economy that would enable the people of New Brunswick to import and purchase the essentials of an affluent way of life, including food. Sacrificing the natural heritage of salmon regeneration on the Wolastoq and the best farmland in the province seemed a reasonable and progressive trade-off to the proponents of the dam.

A few adamant defenders of the river argued against the dam. They lost, but they were right. The dam's headpond destroyed over one hundred kilometres of the Wolastoq's natural ecology and agricultural land between Kingsclear and Woodstock. Fortunately, the promised surge of industrial development did not happen. The dam is now a monument to the tragedy of good intentions.

The dam is now also in trouble. The concrete used to build the powerhouse that holds the generators is unexpectedly deteriorating. It was imagined the dam would last at least one hundred years. At just over fifty years, the structure began to deform in a way that now significantly foreshortens its future. The era of dam removal across North America has arrived. Mactaquac is a prime candidate. The restoration of the Wolastoq is not a fantasy.

With *Atlantis: An Elegy*, George Peabody has given us the inside story of the river in a poem so precisely crafted that comment is superfluous. *Atlantis* is a gift that unfolds in the experience of reading—an experience to which the reader can profitably return again and again.

This poem will outlast and become an elegy for the dam in the literature of place. Although the literature of place always speaks from a particular terrain and time, it speaks as well in tones that resonate across the whole of human experience. The literature of place continually lifts up the human-earth relationship and our sense of home. *Atlantis: An Elegy* is a deeply felt and fully realized contribution to this natural history of our cultural life.

Keith Helmuth, Publisher
Chapel Street Editions
Woodstock, New Brunswick

The QR code below provides access to a recording of the author reading *Atlantis: An Elegy,* courtesy of Andrew and Laura McCain Art Gallery.

https://mccainartgallery.com/atlantis

The reading can also be accessed at a kiosk located on the riverside walkway in Florenceville-Bristol near the Gallery.

About the Author

George Peabody is a lifelong environmental and cultural preservation activist. He is Administrator of the Meduxnekeag River Association, a community based, non-profit, land trust organization in Woodstock, New Brunswick, dedicated to preserving the Appalachian Hardwood Forest and riparian environments of the river's watershed. He is the author of *Schools Days: The One-Room Schools of Maritime Canada*, *Kings Landing: A Living History* and editor of *East Coast Limericks*, and *Best Maritime Short Stories*. He lives alongside the Wolastoq in Lower Woodstock near the site of the original Peabody farm and maintains a market garden at Kirkland. He is preparing a book on the natural and cultural history of the Meduxnekeag River watershed.